This book belongs to:

Published by Ladybird Books Ltd
A Penguin Company
Penguin Books Ltd, 80 Strand, London WC2R 0RL, UK
Penguin Books Australia Ltd, Camberwell, Victoria, Australia
Penguin Books (NZ) Ltd, Private Bag, 102902, NSMC, Auckland 10, New Zealand

5 7 9 10 8 6

ISBN-13: 978-1-84422-281-0
ISBN-10: 1-84422-281-0

Printed in Italy

Dinosaurs

written by Lorraine Horsley
illustrated by Emma Brownjohn

Dinosaurs lived on Earth
millions of years ago.

Brachiosaurus

Compsognathus

Hypsilophodon

Stegosaurus

Allosaurus

Barosaurus

Oviraptor

Parasaurolophus

Baryonyx

Triceratops

7

Some dinosaurs were very small.

Compsognathus was one of the smallest dinosaurs.

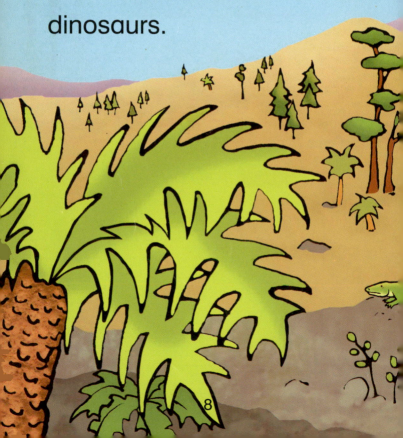

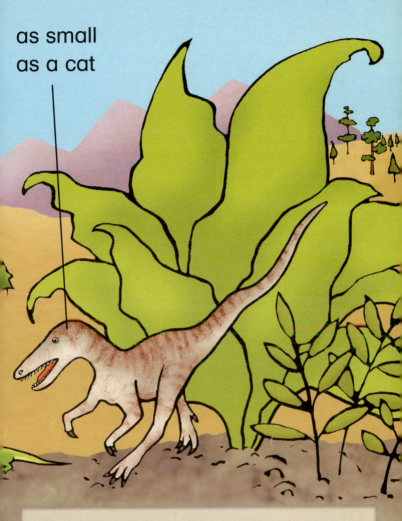

as small
as a cat

Say the name. Comp-sog-nath-us

9

Some dinosaurs were very big.

Brachiosaurus was one of the biggest dinosaurs.

as long as a
tennis court

Say the name. Brak-ee-o-saw-rus

Some dinosaurs were very fast.

Hypsilophodon was one of the fastest dinosaurs.

long legs to
run fast

Say the name. Hip-si-lo-fo-don

Some dinosaurs were very slow.

Stegosaurus was one of the slowest dinosaurs.

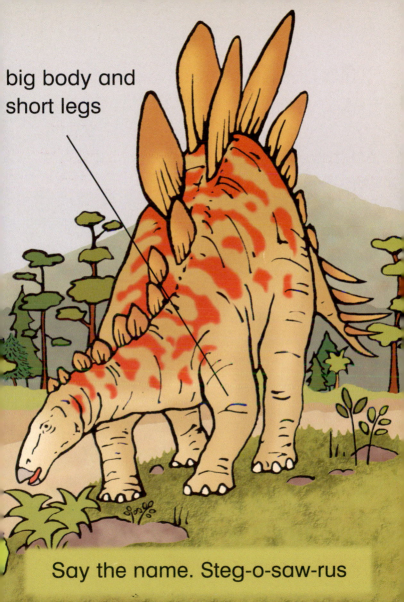

big body and
short legs

Say the name. Steg-o-saw-rus

Some dinosaurs liked to eat plants.

Barosaurus ate the leaves of tall trees.

long neck to
reach leaves

Say the name. Baro-saw-rus

Some dinosaurs liked to
eat eggs.

Oviraptor ate the eggs
of other dinosaurs.

strong beak
to crack eggs

Say the name. O-vee-rap-tor

19

Some dinosaurs liked to eat fish.

Baryonyx ate fish from the rivers.

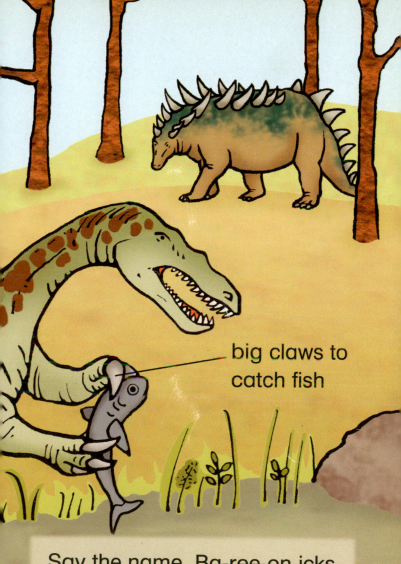

big claws to
catch fish

Say the name. Ba-ree-on-icks

Some dinosaurs liked to eat other dinosaurs.

Allosaurus killed other dinosaurs for food.

sharp claws and
teeth to kill

Say the name. Al-o-saw-rus

Some dinosaurs had
spikes and horns.

Triceratops had
horns to protect itself.

three big
horns for
defence

Say the name. Tri-ser-ra-tops

Some dinosaurs had crests on their heads.

Parasaurolophus had a crest to call other dinosaurs.

crest about one
metre long

Say the name. Pa-ra-saw-rol-off-us

Did you spot these other dinosaurs?

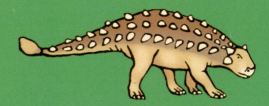

Ankylosaurus

Tyrannosaurus

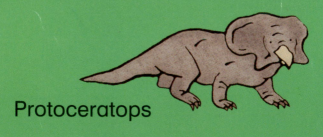

Protoceratops

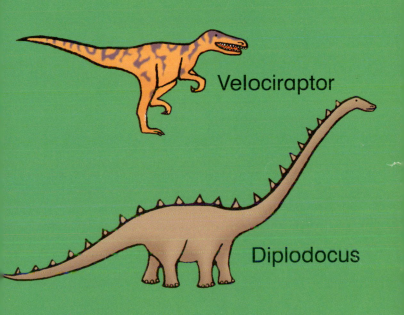

Velociraptor

Diplodocus

Hylaeosaurus

Index